FREDDIE THE FROG™ AND THE MYSTERIOUS WAHOOOOOO

Written by **Sharon Burch**

illustrated by **Tiffany Harris**

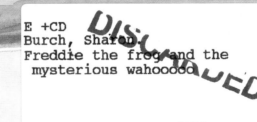

· 3RD ADVENTURE: TEMPO ISLAND ·

MYSTIC PUBLISHING, INC. · Mystic, Iowa

**TO ALEX, WHO WALKS TO HIS OWN STRONG, STEADY BEAT.
THIS ONE'S FOR YOU. LOVE, MOM**
—S.B.

**FOR ROD SCHUCH, THANK YOU FOR INSPIRING ME TO FOLLOW MY
PASSION—I AM ONE OF MANY GRATEFUL STUDENTS.**
—T.H.

---

*This book would not be possible without the incredibly talented team of Tiffany Harris, Deborah Watley,
Grant Wood, Jonathan White, Kim Adlerman, Danny Adlerman, and my indispensable Bill Burch.
Go team! Thanks for making Freddie look and sound good. You rock!*

Printed in China.
Book design and production by *The Kids at Our House*.
The artwork in *Freddie the Frog™ and The Mysterious Wahooooo* rendered in watercolor, acrylic, and pen and ink on watercolor paper.

The sound track on the audio CD accompanying *Freddie the Frog™ and The Mysterious Wahooooo* was composed and performed by Grant Wood and Jonathan White.
Narration and character voices by Jonathan White.

Publisher's Cataloging-in-Publication (Provided by Quality Books, Inc.)

    Burch, Sharon (Sharon Kay)
       Freddie the frog and the mysterious wahooooo / written by Sharon Burch ; illustrated by Tiffany Harris.
       p. cm. + 1 sound disc (digital ; 4 3/4 in.). — (3rd adventure. Tempo Island)
       Includes compact disc.
       SUMMARY: Freddie the frog and Eli the elephant discover rhythm, beat and tempo on Tempo Island, where they meet new musical friends
         that speak a different language.
       Audience: Ages 3-9.
       LCCN 2007903051
       ISBN-13: 978-0-9747454-7-3
       ISBN 0-9747454-7-2

    1. Frogs—Juvenile fiction. 2. Elephants—Juvenile fiction. 3. Music—Juvenile fiction. [1. Frogs—Fiction. 2. Elephants—Fiction. 3. Music—Fiction.]
      I. Harris, Tiffany, ill. II. Title. III. Title: Mysterious wahooooo.

    PZ7.B91586Mys 2007   [E]
                 QBI07-600177 (Provided by Quality Books, Inc.)

"Cowabunga!"

"Wow! What a ride!" exclaimed Eli.

"Yeah!" panted Freddie.
"But look at our raft! How are we going to get home?"

"WAHOOOOO!" called a deep voice, beyond the trees.
"WAHOOOOO!" echoed two other voices.
"What was that?" asked Freddie.

"It sounded like an elephant trumpet," said Eli.
"Look!" Freddie pointed above the trees.
A flock of birds was flying in big circles in the sky. The birds kept going around and around and around.
"What are they doing?" Eli said.

"ANDANTE!" called the deep voice.
"ANDANTE!"

"Andante? What does that mean?" Freddie asked Eli. Suddenly, the birds dove through the trees. Then Freddie and Eli heard....

BOOM, BOOM, BOOM, BOOM, BOOM, BOOM, BOOM, BOOM

Eli thumped his huge feet with the steady beat.

"Shh!" Freddie said. "Listen." Eli stopped thumping and lifted his ears. Now they heard someone chanting a catchy rhythm.

TI-TI, TA, TI-TI, TA

Freddie's webbed feet began to wiggle and kick.
He couldn't keep them still. Then his whole body
broke out into a dance. What kind of island was this?
    "FINE!" the deep voice roared suddenly.
    "FINE!" Everything stopped—even Freddie and Eli.

Then the two friends entered the jungle. "We've got to find out who is making this music!" Eli said.

The elephant call sounded again.

"WAHOOOOO!"

"WAHOOOOO!"

Up went the birds, circling and circling.

"ALLEGRO!" called the deep voice.

"ALLEGRO!"

Again, the birds dove through the trees, and the same beat began, but faster.

BOOM, BOOM, BOOM, BOOM, BOOM, BOOM, BOOM, BOOM

Oooooh! Eli could not resist thumping the beat. Freddie crouched between Eli's ears, listening. Would there be another rhythm?

TI-TI, TI-TI, TI-TI, TA

Freddie yelled, "Let's boogie!" He kicked his skinny legs, flung his arms, and swung to the rhythm.
"TI-TI, TI-TI, TI-TI, TA..."
"FINE!" called the deep voice.
"FINE!"
The music stopped.

As Freddie and Eli forced their way through the trees and bushes, they heard the trumpeting again.

"WAHOOOOO!"
"WAHOOOOO!"
Up soared the birds.
Down fell Freddie.
"LARGO!"
"LARGO!"
Down dropped the birds. The bass line beat thumped slowly.

BOOM, BOOM, BOOM, BOOM, BOOM, BOOM, BOOM, BOOM

Freddie scrambled back on top of Eli just before Eli's feet began pounding the ground.

TI-KA-TI-KA, TA, TI-KA-TI-KA, TA

Freddie liked this rhythm! He bounced
his shoulders and kicked his feet.
He chanted, too.
**"TI-KA-TI-KA, TA, TI-KA-TI-KA, TA,
TI-KA-TI-KA, TA, TI-KA-TI-KA, TA..."**
"FINE!"
"FINE!"
Everything stopped.

Eli and Freddie pushed aside a huge leaf. They found the
colorful birds sitting on the head of a purple elephant!
And Freddie and Eli saw a bobaloo baboon and an
orangutan-tang.

"**WAHOOOOO!**" the purple elephant trumpeted.
"**WAHOOOOO!**" echoed the bobaloo baboon and
the orangutan-tang.

The birds dropped to the ground, picked up sticks, and hovered over the trio.

"PRESTO!"
"PRESTO!"

The purple elephant began thumping a fast beat on his upright bass.

BOOM, BOOM, BOOM, BOOM, BOOM, BOOM, BOOM, BOOM

The birds swooped down and laid
their sticks in a pattern. They were
playing a game!

"TA, TA, TA, SHH,"
chanted the bobaloo baboon.
The orangutan-tang's large hands
slapped the rhythm on a drum.

Freddie and Eli imitated the trio. But the two friends didn't notice the ground crumbling under Eli's pounding feet. Suddenly, the sandy bluff gave way and Freddie and Eli tumbled down.

They landed right in the middle of the animals!

"Mi scusi," said the purple elephant.

"Excuse me?" Eli said.

"Mi capisce?" asked the purple elephant.

Freddie scratched his head.

"TIKA, TIKA, TIKA, TIKA," twittered the birds.

Freddie talked slowly and used hand motions. "I'm Freddie, and this is Eli. Eli and I live on Treble Clef Island."

"May we join you?" asked Eli. The animals and birds just stared at him. They did not understand. Then Eli had an idea.

Eli raised his small trunk and trumpeted with all his might, **"WAHOOOOO!"**
"WAHOOOOO!" responded Freddie.
Eli thumped a slow, largo beat.

BOOM, BOOM, BOOM, BOOM, BOOM, BOOM, BOOM, BOOM

The island creatures smiled. Music! They understood!
The birds quickly laid a new rhythm on the ground.
Freddie danced and chanted.

TI-TI, TI-TI, TA, TA

Eli thumped a little faster.
"ACCELERANDO!" exclaimed the purple elephant.
"ACCELERANDO!" echoed all the others.

The purple elephant plucked his bass, matching Eli's beat. The orangutan-tang played the rhythm on his drum. And the bobaloo baboon joined Freddie, chanting and dancing to the rhythm. The elephants increased the tempo to

ANDANTE....

Then **ALLEGRO....**

And finally, **PRESTO**, until the animals could not stay together any longer.

"**RITARDANDO!**" yelled the purple elephant.

"**RITARDANDO!**"

The elephants began to slow the beat.

Freddie led them in a conga line back to the other side
of the island.

"FINE!"
"FINE!"

Everyone stopped. They looked
around at each other and laughed.
Together they had made a
great song!

Then Freddie pointed to the raft
pieces scattered over the beach.
    "Will you help us get home?"
Freddie asked. He pointed to Treble
Clef Island.

The purple elephant,
bobaloo baboon, and
orangutan-tang nodded, "Sì."
   "WAHOOOOO!"
exclaimed the purple elephant.
   "WAHOOOOO!" the rest of the
animals shouted. They gathered the raft
pieces, and the birds found vines to tie
the wood together. As the new friends
worked, they hummed their song.

"Wow! Thanks!" exclaimed Freddie. "That was fun!"
He slapped the baboon a high-five.

Then, Freddie
and Eli paddled away from the island.
     "Ciao!" called their new friends, waving good-bye.
     "Ciao!" echoed Freddie and Eli.

Freddie and Eli sang all the way home.
"TI-TI, TI-TI, TA, TA, TI-TI, TI-TI, TA, TA..."

TEMPO ISLAND CONGA

Lyrics by Sharon Burch, Jonathan White, and Grant Wood
Music by Grant Wood

Come on, do the Conga!
The Tempo Island Conga!
Stand up on your feet—
Form a line of people.
Roll your arms and kick right.
Roll your arms and kick left.
Step three times and kick right.
Step three times and kick left.
Come on, do the Conga!
The Tempo Island Conga!

Freddie and Eli discovered Italian words that describe music.

Tempo = speed of the music
Andante = walking tempo
Allegro = quick and lively tempo
Largo = very slow tempo
Presto = very fast tempo
Accelerando = gradually increase the tempo
Ritardando = gradually decrease the tempo

Other music words:

Beat = the steady pulse felt in music

Rhythm = patterns of short and long sounds in music

♩ = *ta* = quarter note

♫ = *ti-ti* = two eighth notes

♬♬ = *ti-ka-ti-ka* = four sixteenth notes

𝄽 = *shh* = quarter rest

𝄆   𝄇 = repeat sign

MUSIC LESSONS
IN
FREDDIE THE FROG™ AND THE MYSTERIOUS WAHOOOOO

- **TEMPO TERMS:** *largo, andante, allegro, presto, fine, accelerando, and ritardando*
- **BEAT:** Identifying and playing the beat in music
- **RHYTHM:** Reading, performing, and creating using the **MAGNETIC RHYTHM SET** (sold separately)
- **BEAT VS. RHYTHM:** Understanding the difference between beat and rhythm

JAM TRACK FUN!

Practice playing **BEAT** and **RHYTHM** using rhythm instruments and the enclosed **AUDIO CD**:

BEAT

1. **PLAY JAM TRACKS** 5, 6, 7, or 8.
2. **PRACTICE** the beat with each track.

RHYTHM

1. **CREATE** a new four-count rhythm pattern using the **MAGNETIC RHYTHM SET** (sold separately).
2. **PRACTICE** your new rhythm.
3. **PLAY JAM TRACKS** 5, 6, 7, or 8.
4. **PRACTICE** your new rhythm with each track.

A RHYTHM BAND! In a group setting, divide the children into a **"BEAT"** group and a **"RHYTHM"** group to form a rhythm band. Success Tip: First, practice groups separately. Second, practice groups together with the largo track. Then, jam with faster tracks!

More **TEACHING IDEAS** at: www.freddiethefrogbooks.com